D0491112

BURNING WIRE

Ruth Fainlight was born in New York City, and has lived mostly in England since the age of 15. Her father was born in London, and her mother in a small town on the eastern borders of the Austro-Hungarian Empire (now in Ukraine). She was educated at schools in America and England, and at Birmingham and Brighton colleges of art, and married the writer Alan Sillitoe in 1959. She was Poet in Residence at Vanderbilt University, Nashville, Tennessee, in 1985 and 1990, and received a Cholmondeley Award for Poetry in 1994.

Her many books include poetry, short stories, translations, drama and opera libretti. Her poems have appeared in numerous anthologies, and her stories in books including *The Penguin Book of Modern Women's Stories* (1991) and *Caught in a Story: contemporary fairy-tales and fables* (Vintage, 1992).

Her poetry books include: *Cages* (1966) and *To See the Matter Clearly* (1968), from Macmillan in Britain and Dufour in the USA; *The Region's Violence* (1973), *Another Full Moon* (1976), *Sibyls and Others* (1980), *Fifteen to Infinity* (1983), *Selected Poems* (1987) and *The Knot* (1990), all from Hutchinson and Century Hutchinson; *This Time of Year* (1994) and *Selected Poems* (1995) from Sinclair-Stevenson; and *Climates* (1983), *Sugar-Paper Blue* (1997) and *Burning Wire* (2002) from Bloodaxe Books. *Fifteen to Infinity* was published in the USA by Carnegie Mellon University Press. *Sugar-Paper Blue* was shortlisted for the Whitbread Poetry Award.

She has also translated two books of poetry from the Portuguese of Sophia de Mello Breyner, and collaborated with Alan Sillitoe on *All Citizens Are Soldiers*, a translation of Lope de Vega's play *Fuenteovejuna*. Her own poetry has been published in Portuguese (1995), French (1997) and Spanish (2000) editions.

She has published two collections of short stories, *Daylife and Nightlife* (André Deutsch, 1971) and *Dr Clock's Last Case* (Virago, 1994). Her libretti include: *The Dancer Hotoke* (1991), a chamber opera by Erika Fox (nominated for the Laurence Oliver Awards in 1992); *The European Story* (1993), a chamber opera by Geoffrey Alvarez; and *Bedlam Britannica* (1995), a Channel Four *War Cries* TV opera directed by Celia Lowenstein with music by Robert Jan Stips.

RUTH FAINLIGHT

Burning Wire

BLOODAXE BOOKS

ISBN: 1 85224 597 2

First published 2002 by
Bloodaxe Books Ltd,
Highgreen,
Tarset,
Northumberland NE48 1RP.

www.bloodaxebooks.com
For further information about Bloodaxe titles
please visit our website or write to
the above address for a catalogue.

Bloodaxe Books Ltd acknowledges
the financial assistance of Northern Arts.

(23.09.02) c.

Cover printing by J. Thomson Colour Printers Ltd, Glasgow.

Printed in Great Britain by
Cromwell Press Ltd, Trowbridge, Wiltshire.

Acknowledgements

Acknowledgements and thanks are due to the editors of the following publications in which some of these poems first appeared: *Acumen*, *Around the Globe* (Globe Theatre), *Five Points* (USA), *The Hudson Review* (USA), *The Jerusalem Review*, *Jewish Quarterly*, *New Statesman*, *New Writing 10* (Picador/The British Council, 2001), *PN Review*, *Poetry London*, *Poetry Review*, *The Rialto*, *The Southern Review* (USA), *Tabacaria* (Casa Fernando Pessoa, Lisbon), *Thumbscrew*, *The Times Literary Supplement* and *The Threepenny Review* (USA).

'An Encounter in Ladbroke Square' and 'In Ladbroke Square' are from a sequence, *Time and Ladbroke Square*, commissioned by the Poetry Society for use on their website as part of their Poetry Places programme.

'Black', 'Four Pheasants', 'Feathers', 'Feathers and Jug', 'The Constellation of the Jacket', 'The Coloration of Feathers' and 'The Second Page' are the text of *Feathers*, an artist's book with mezzotints by Judith Rothchild, published by Éditions Veridgris, Octon, France. 'The Begonias' is one of the poems from *Leaves/Feuilles*, an artist's book with mezzotints by Judith Rothchild, published by Éditions Verdigris.

The sequence *Sheba and Solomon* is the text of an artist's book with hand-coloured drypoints by Ana Maria Pacheco, published by Pratt Contemporary Art.

Contents

Burning Wire

I *The Medium*

Rein back from thought until
you are its medium – or
force mind forward like
a burning wire into the core
of question, explore the process
of release and tension.

The medium is ink
and paper, the product, you hope
– holding your breath before
you dare to judge the simplest
word or metaphor –
is something like a poem.

II *The Nightingale*

I was hoping the nightingale would go somewhere else, sing
outside another window – then

had to laugh at myself, as I groped for my earplugs. I tried
to get back to sleep, but the nightingale

forced its song like a cauterising wire into the dark,
demanding a poem.

In the Dream

In the dream I was an old, smiling woman
– like one of those Japanese wise men
(squat-bodied, knotty-limbed, head tilting back
as if to make eye-contact with something
only he can see above him in the sky)
you might find in a woodblock print.

In the dream I was as free as they.
Decades of tension and vanity had slid like
a silken cloak off my shoulders. Now,
the coarse weave of my dress was faded and worn,
garb of a pilgrim or hermit (though others
moved beside me on the road, through the market),
and I knew this was a crucial moment: when
I woke I could choose – for the rest of my life
if I wished – to be that woman.

Song

The brush of something heavy and wet
                    against your leg in passing
a rustle behind your back a flicker
                    in the corner of your eye
like an uneasy awareness you don't
                    want to acknowledge
a weariness and impatience
                    with the repetition
of energy and ambition, always new
                    theories, life-forms, styles...

It's like the ocean, processions of waves
                    cresting the horizon
moving towards you. If only you could sink
                    down through the gritty sand
and opalescent pebbles
                    deep enough not to return.
The dirty foam at the edge of the tide
                    is the hem of a coat
dragged across the beach by a figure
                    who might be from the future
receding with a courtly flourish...
                    better to smile than cry.

Transience

Like a flock of pigeons
settling on the roof ridge
opposite before they
lift off and wheel around
again: the raucous flutter
the shimmer of eyes and wings...

Like a flush of fruit flies
in the momentary season
of their existence...

Like coals in a furnace:
that throb as if a giant sighed
the low rush of breath
through massive lungs
and the halo of burning gas
colourless at the surface
mercury white, then
methane blue and yellow
as it flares and dulls...

Like a surge of water,
prismatic reflections and
widening circles on the
rocking meniscus shivered
when the tension is broken
by one of the stones: each
a different shape and colour...

Like the compulsion
of the one who throws it...

...Whichever image,
contrast or analogy you
choose, for transience.

Ephemeral Lives

This year seems an interlude
between two events, though I don't yet know
what those events are. The first
must already have happened (at the time
I didn't notice), but until the second,
whenever it comes, the future stays obscure.

A week now is as short as a day,
a month no longer than a week used to be.
The only way to stop acceleration
(this hopeful theory still needs testing)
would be to concentrate my attention
on the smallest details of a fly, a mouse,
a flower. Compared to such ephemeral lives,
my own will proceed with glacial slowness.

Beetle

In the sealed gap between the inner and outer
window (neither of which can be opened)
of the downstairs cloakroom – a large dark beetle.

For a long time I watched this investigation
of its prison's limits, the effort to climb
the thin leaded edge of the bar dividing
the outer window into smaller panes.

But impossible to get a purchase on
glass or metal: after each effort, straining
upward a few inches, it topples backwards.

At last, after the six thin jointed legs
had flailed, bicycling helplessly, like the limbs
of bodies falling through space, somehow
it rights itself and struggles back to its feet.

There is a pause, as if mustering strength,
a posture of tenacity, what seems a stare
of stubborn hope. Then the process starts again.

I do not want to monitor its death.
But unless I break the window, I cannot
release it or myself. Then the beetle-god
blesses us both; next morning, the space is empty.

What

What was God doing
through cycles of aeons
as the planet steadied and cooled
elements were captured
matter shifted and fused,
before even the first creature
first amoeba, first mammal...

Was he brooding on the waters
face turned away, endlessly
patient, secure in his purpose
between storm and eruption
while the heavens formed and
evolution slowly produced
the consciousness of worshippers...

The faith demanded from humans
is nothing, compared to
the fissions of energy needed
to sustain belief
in his own existence, endure
the darkness, the silence
the purgatorial waiting, waiting...

Imagine the moment
that affirmed his being, when the first
prayer rose to his gratified ear,
smoke and fumes
from the sacrificial fire,
as his doubts were banished
his obstinacy justified...

And what, since then, has God been doing?

Thankful

Nothing ever happens more than once.
The next time is never like before.
What you thought you learned doesn't apply.
Something is different. And just as real.
For which you might be thankful after all.

The Tree Surgeon

Pressing against the trunk, he twists around
and back to test the resilience of the branch,
the rope, the safety of his position,
then crawls along a bough – a primate
in his habitat. When he stops to rest and
contemplate the distracting criss-cross of last
season's twigs, plot his next move and where
to cut yet not harm the tree's structure,
he becomes again a modern human.

Next spring it will start again. By autumn,
when this year's leaves have fallen, the space
he's cleared will be filigreed with new growth.
The pressure of a tool on his palm, the timeless
repetitions of toil, seem part of the same
process: something more important than
an individual life. He's caring for trees,
not carving a sculpture that will immortalise
him; would never conceive such ambitions.

At ground level, two men, helmeted,
their ears muffled against the sound, feed
fallen branches through the mouth of a hopper
that spits the shredded stuff into the open back
of a truck. The tree surgeon, gracefully
stretching toward the tip of the tallest branch,
is only not an artist because he knows
that what he does could be done as well –
or maybe even better – by someone else.

Ordinary Sorrow

'Mozart touched that piece of paper,' he said,
'wrote music on it, and now I touched it.'
This was a young man talking – awestruck,
overwhelmed – feeling another power
for the first time. His excitement was touching.

Mozart, in *Così*, Shakespeare in the *Dream*,
knew enough not to judge such miracles,
call this one a hero or villain, nor
think themselves more immune than kings, lovers
or fools to ordinary joy and sorrow.

They shared the objectivity of gods
towards their own lives as much as others',
the tender amusement that defines wisdom.
Beauty's vivid favourites, and death's
levelled ranks, were what touched them most.

Potatoes

A young woman sits in the stone-flagged kitchen, the bowl of potatoes she is peeling for the family dinner in front of her on the scrubbed wooden table. Like every other day, she is meticulously cutting away the eyes and specks of rot from their pale raw flesh.

In one chilblained hand, chapped fingers and split thumb-ends engrained with kitchen dirt, she holds the angular half of a peeled potato, in the other, a small steel paring knife so old that it had been her mother's favourite, the blade worn thin and crescent-shaped.

Lifting both arms high to her narrow chest and pressing them against the ache inside as she stifles a cough, she moves into the patch of wintry morning light that lies like a frozen puddle below the small high window, squinting myopic eyes with the effort to see more clearly.

Her sister peers around, then softly shuts, the kitchen door. Too abrupt a waking might block the soul's re-entry into its vacant body. She knows that Emily is far away, out on the moor.

Prosody

Tone alters. Words sound different
now, transmute in the alembic
of iambic – whichever structure
the image chooses as its form:
trochee's fused aggression,
pyrrhic's fluid modesty.
Thought is fractured into dactyls
or confirmed by anapaest,
while special pleading, argument
and rhetoric prefer spondees.
Slowly, you become more fluent
in this new language. Springing
rhythms lift your limbs in dance.
Ancestors speak through your mouth.

This Visitor

A white night, a cold dawn, London
mid-October. After months
of blindness, dumbness, this visitor
and her confirming song.

She stood tranquil and tall
strong toes gripping the ground
head wrapped in a pale green cloth
wearing a faded blue gown.

The sidelong shrewd glance
of grey eyes under smooth brows
assessed me but was not hostile.
I knew I had passed a test

when she stepped forward, away
from the others, laid
a small warm hand on my arm
led me toward her house.

After months of blindness, dumbness,
such confirmation.

Footprint

You are cast away
in a damaged boat, the unmapped ocean
empty to the horizon

to glide beneath a wall
of ashy cliffs, till past a headland
a harbour slyly opens.

Quickly, swing the tiller
press the paddle deep and hard
push through the reef towards

that track of smoother water
marked like moirèd silk or oil-slick
on a darker surface

across the waves' rhythm
calm against their raucous tumult
the current's counterpoint

until the splintered boat
is safely beached. Your footprint
will not be the first.

Insistence

I never thought I would be writing about the moon
                                                      at my age
nor that a full moon could still keep me awake,
                                        restless, excited,
all through a summer's night, like the old days.

But this insistent moon, bright rock in a dark sky,
                                        blatantly present
when the curtains are parted, demands response.
                                        For one moment
I am confused, uncertain, a girl again.

Then confident as she, return that gaze.
                                        To such insistence
that nothing has changed, I reaffirm my role and
                                        fate: to be
a watchful, solitary sister of the moon.

Black

A crow
in the middle of the road
a brushstroke marking a word
on an opened scroll
in a script I cannot read

that only lifts
as I approach
at the last moment
with a sudden clap of wings
abrupt, its mission done:

to search me out
on this empty stretch
of pale winter road, with
a summons from a black-
beaked, bird-masked god.

La Chaise Bleue

(for Judith Rothchild & her picture 'La Chaise Bleue')

Shadows are moving across a wall
of pale stone and crumbling mortar –
an image of coolness, like running water
or darkness inside an open door.

The rustle of wind through dusty lime leaves,
a shutter's intermittent creak
and the cicadas' stridor, seem
voices choiring the noonday heat.

Upstairs in the bedroom, under
a beamed ceiling, two lovers,
smooth bodies pungent
with sweat and perfume, turn from each other.

Poised between the house and terrace,
its angled legs as delicate
as an insect hovering above the threshold,
the blue chair stands empty.

Feathers

You came back from the market
with a fresh-killed chicken,
barely plucked.
It still felt warm.

Inside the carcass,
the butcher had stuffed
feet, head, heart, crest,
liver and gizzard
and other bits I didn't
recognise: raw
crimson, watery pink
and livid blue, already
varnished by death-fluids.

The yellow skin, pale
as a sodden lemon husk
in a glass of cold tea, was pocked
and shadowed by horny sheaths
of half-extracted quills
and dark filaments
of broken feathers,
like an unshaved face.
I worried them out with tweezers.

When my mother cleaned a chicken,
after she'd sluiced and patted
it dry, she held it over
the gas stove's burner
for a final singeing.
I remember the stink
of scorched feathers. Now,
above a glowing brasier,
we tried to do it right.

Later that night, in bed,
a pillow split. The air

was thick with down and feathers.
They stuck to our lips
floated up as we laughed
and would not settle. You said
I seemed to have wings. I wanted
every bristle of your beard
to sprout a feather.

Our Song

Stripped vine-stocks, leaves gone red and yellow
and every beaten-copper, crumpled-leather
shade between: the beauties of decay.
(Sweetheart, that's our song! Play it again!)

Primrose Cottage

A rattling latch against a dark oak door
at the bottom of the crooked stairs.

Swathes of misty rain blown from the west
blurred the panes until we barely saw

early windfalls rotting in the uncut grass,
fly-infested doilies of Queen Anne's lace.

Thorn needles and heavy 78s: 'His
Master's Voice'; a wind-up Victrola in a

dusty corner. A Turkish carpet with
faded motifs and tangled fringes, worn at the edge.

We tried to light a fire in the low-ceilinged bedroom's
shallow grate with the last slack but it made us choke –

so kissed, laughed, and dragged each other back
into the sagging bed and damp sheets.

Sunday Afternoon

A Sunday afternoon in late July:
the leaves look tired, the sky is clouding up,
pressure falling. The couple
in the next apartment are arguing
about how much he does or doesn't help.
Eavesdropping from my terrace,
I am jealous of how it's bound to end:
the stuffy bedroom, moans and love-cries muffled
so the baby won't wake.
I remember every detail of
the misery there is in marriage –
and then making up.

Four Pheasants

Where the road curves sharp left, it dips,
and after heavy rain, a glisten of wet –
what might be the bed of an old stream or
an overflowing spring – marks the surface.
The water sinks into the dark earth
deepened by centuries of rotting leaves
and decomposing creatures, and the trees arch.
Their top branches meet above the gap.

When the leaves are russet and gold, the wet road,
fitfully lit by weak sunlight filtered through
interlaced twigs, seems to lead somewhere important.
From a bank of bronze and copper bracken,
dew-beaded, frost-softened, four pheasants
emerge, one behind the next, and stalk across.

The Drive Back

A line of speckled white and black cows
evenly spaced: baked Egyptian funerary beads
strung on a necklace.

The tenacity of hedges
which keep growing back,
no matter how drastic the treatment they get.

Spiky rows of pale stubble
shifting angles as we round the corner.
A house of cards collapsing on a brown table.

Ragged grey clouds rear up over a road sign:
Welcome to Wiltshire.
The sun goes in like a light switched off.

Harsh filigree of bare trees
at the top of a hill. When the sun shone,
mottled patterns of bark and leaves and

green stains of moss on their trunks
clung soft as camouflage-net, but a change of light
hammers them to iron silhouettes.

Passing Stonehenge. Last week, it stood squat
and black under anvils of cumulo-nimbus.
Today, rises pallid from a surf of tourists.

The English Country Cottage

A Jewish poet in an English village:
incongruous and inappropriate
as a Hindu in an igloo, a Dayak in
Chicago, a giraffe at the South Pole.

That shadowy yew in the churchyard, only
a few steps away from this cottage door,
was planted in the centuries between
the Lincoln pogrom (when little St Hugh,
they claimed, was murdered by the Jews, and all
Christ-killers left alive were banished)
and the year when Oliver Cromwell changed the law
to grant honourable men of Israelite persuasion,
with their prudent wives and obedient children,
the privilege to be legally present in England.

As a youth, my father was a patriot,
a Labour-voting true blue. But though
he felt entirely English, the problem was:
to certain natives of whatever class
he was a wily, greasy Levantine
and always would be. His solution was
to leave the country, go far enough away
to 'pass for white', somewhere he could play
at being pukka-English through and through.
(Yet still more proud to be a Jew.)

Maybe because she came from Bukovina,
my mother had no illusions. She was used to
rejection, born to it. First, the shock
of Ellis Island: another world, another
language (I knew how hard she tried). Then
further uprooting; though the nineteen thirties
were not exactly propitious, her restless husband
– handsome, dreamy, unpolitical –
felt the lure of home, dragged her to England.

I ran straight into the fire's centre,
towards the focus of trouble, glamour, danger;
danced, like Esmeralda, on the Round Table
as desperately as if to save my life.
Such were my tactics in those distant times.
Now (though mimicking the locals dutifully),
thatch and cruck-beams cannot camouflage
the alien. The carillon rings mockery.

Sometimes I wonder if I should have known better:
to sweetly smile and eat the mess
of pottage – but never sell my birthright
for an English country cottage.

Green Tomatoes

Down the high street, past the post box,
Doris, whose husband suddenly died
at the weekend, called me over. She was
mowing the lawn to make it all tidy
before the funeral. Arms and legs
bare in the heat, skin sagging
like washed-out, faded longjohns,
she led me into the steamy warmth of
a greenhouse crowded with green tomatoes
as hard and vivid as malachite.
'Would you like some?' she asked.
                    'They won't stop ripening.'

An Encounter Near Ladbroke Square

A windy, rainy night, about eleven o'clock.
A small moon half hidden by ragged cloud.
He puffed a cigar, strolling back from the club
along a new-made road in what were still
the western outskirts, pondering adventure.

In the long intervals between the gas lights
he wondered if he were safe. Then he saw a policeman
and called a loud goodnight. The fresh coarse gravel
on footpath and carriageway crunched under his feet.
The noise disturbed him. He stepped onto the meadowland.

At the end of the lamps, an empty row of new-built houses.
Their garden walls loomed gaunt above the open field.
He turned the corner sharply.
Out of the blackness a woman approached.
He slowed, and clinked the coins in his waistcoat pocket.

She wore a big round hat with a dirty feather,
a dark dress with a small shawl across her breast,
a clean white apron, white stockings, and strong boots.
She was tallish, thick-set, and looked about thirty,
like a woman who sold things from a barrow in Notting Dale.

In Ladbroke Square

The oldest trees have
boughs strong as elephants' legs
bark gnarled as their hide.

Under their branches
generations of children
insects, flowers, vines.

(In the trees' shadow
children tear blossom apart
rip the wings off flies.)

The Begonias

Don Carlos de Begonia,
grand old navigator,
the monarch's favourite –
his wattled neck is weathered
by salt and sun to the red
of watered blood and glistens
with stubble like silver
filigree or Aztec crystal.

II

Doña Angel de Begonia
wears a long collar
spotted with white and pink
rosettes. With lowered eyes
and folded hands, she prays
that sober demeanour and secret
penance will gain remission
for her father's sins.

Lisbon Faces

The cats on the azulejos
of the Fronteira palace,
the putti, birds and satyrs –
cobalt blue and manganese
black, with yellow eyes,

the fishermen and monks, Jews
and courtiers, the royal pair
with ornate rich-toned robes,
honouring São Vicente
in Nuno Gonçalves' painting,

have a subtle resemblance – that
shrewd, mournful, watchful expression –
to people I passed in Alfama
this morning: they all share
the same Lisbon face.

Peruvian Views
(for Mimi and Moisés)

I *Over N.W. Peru*

Are those clouds, or snowy mountain peaks?
I think they might be both. And
the thin, white, broken line I see,
peering through the smeared plane window
to where a heaped swirl of dun rock and
sand, streaked by the dry trails
of ancient meanders, meets green ocean
must be moving surf – though from
thirty thousand feet seems as fixed
as the horizon's distance
      and bright immensity.

II *Amazon*

Glare then darkness. Indurated lianas.
The feel of shallow laterite underfoot.
The clammy heat the racket

and that other pressure: totally focussed existence
one thing clutching onto growing into another
a tree's tensed roots thrusting out from its trunk
like buttresses to arch over reach further
straining to claim some untouched patch of ground
to draw whatever nourishment has not
been leached yet by the rain – the crazy
struggle for *lebensraum*
for light and air and space.

Mottle freckle iridescence maculation
on strident insect furtive reptile raucous
brilliant bird or scurrying hot-blooded creature.
Whistle. Grunt. Moan. Roar. Shriek.
The code and language of compulsions
you will not confront
    cannot ignore
        are not allowed to forget.

III *At Huacachina Oasis*

Tamarisk, bamboo, eucalyptus, palm,
an opal-green lagoon. How soft the air seems
here – not like the parching desert glare
of wind-paled dunes that rear above the trees.

Scrape mud from the water's edge, take it
back to Lima to make a mask for your face,
and you will stay – perhaps even become,
the legend goes – as beautiful

as the Inca princess who drowned herself
for love in these smooth oasis waters.
Now, she rises with the moon's reflection

to sing her story and lure young swimmers
under the opaque oily surface towards
her embrace: the mermaid of Huacachina.

IV *El Niño*

A thousand years used to seem nothing,
the blink of a pterodactyl's eye.
I could cast my mind back an epoch or two
without even having to try.

Now I find it hard to imagine
more than a decade into the future.
Is it the end of the century, the world,
or my own life that blocks the view?

Apocalyptic dreams and fears confuse the issue,
while a steaming dragon-tongue of ocean laps Peru.

Montevideo

Cabbalistic calculations and lists of numbers on the pasteboard back of a photograph – pencil scrawls in a rapid hand; and up toward the right top corner a faded blue, oval-shaped stamp: '*The Hughes Business College and Academy of Languages*, 1476 Treinta y Tres [1833: the date of a battle in the independence wars, commemorated by the name of the boulevard], Montevideo.' But when she looked for that address, that street and building, fifty years later, she could not find them.

She recognises him at once, on the edge of the group. That pretty girl is his sister Fanny. Whether the stocky man nearby is her grandfather she can't be sure. No one is still alive who could tell her what they were doing, why they are included, whether teachers or students. Serious-faced, swarthy and fair, respectably dressed and combed, children and women are seated in rows, men standing behind, posed against a wall on a wide terrace: perhaps the picture taken at the end of each school year, or as the souvenir of an excursion.

Her not-yet aunt and prospective father already show the family face: the shared curve of lips and wary, attentive eyes, a combination of arrogance, insecurity and charm. Not having noted such a resemblance before, she is shocked by how much they look like her son, as he turned to say goodbye, then left for Montevideo.

Crushed Geraniums

(for H.B.)

The pungent reek of marigolds
strung around a black-faced idol's neck,
the sweet decay of sacrificial blood
mixed with rotting orange petals smeared
across an altar at the Kalighat.
There is the acetone of anguish, the gush
of phenol triggered by fear or lust, but

what was the source of the crushed-geranium scent
which always comes when she remembers, always
brings it back: sight/sound/smell/
pity//////horror:
          that day she followed
          the exhausted, disbelieving victors
          into Belsen camp.

Shocked

(i.m. F.M.)

How few expressions a face adopts,
are even possible. Muscles
tighten or relax in combinations
of the same features – whether
to laugh or groan or sob. To read
its meaning, you need the context.

That look of amazement
brows raised and eyes rounded
mouth held pursed forward
with closed lips presenting
for a kiss or to repress – what
wordless recognition?

I hadn't seen that face since we met
forty years before, days
after her marriage, until here
in a hospital ward, after
the operation, where she waits
for the biopsy results.

The same expression: shocked
by fear or delight (now she
has met the gaze of both
that pair, Love & Death), back
to the core of her obstinately
unalterable self.

The Clarinettist

Pale round arms raising her clarinet
at the exact angle, she sways, then halts,
poised for the music

like a horse that gathers itself up before the leap
with the awkward, perfect, only
possible movement

an alto in a quattrocento chorus, blond head
lifted from the score, open mouthed
for hallelujah

a cherub on a ceiling cornice leaning out
from heaped-up clouds of opalescent pink,
translucent blue

a swimmer breasting frothy surf like ripping through
lace curtains, a dancer centred as a spinning top,
an August moon

alone, in front of the orchestra, the conductor's
other, and unacknowledged opposite,
she starts the tune.

Opera in Holland Park

Raucous peacocks like abandoned babies
counterpoint the final chorus of *Tosca*, Act I.

Every table in the café is occupied
by drinkers halted in the posture of listeners:
abstracted gaze, alertly lifted head.

The fumy blaze of flowerbeds, smouldering braziers
in the summer dusk. Vortices of midges
vibrate above the hedges like heat mirages.

To stare at the waterfall in the Japanese garden
for more than a few moments alters the scale:
a thousand-metre plunge down an Andean precipice.

In the interval, the audience eat ice cream, stroll
past the orangery. Violinists tighten their strings.

I have never been so close to a peacock before.
It struts, stops, opens its beak, emits a creaking,
tentative call and makes me jump with fright.

The small blue head swivels, crowned by feather-antennae
searching a signal. Precise articulation of
spurred legs like precious mottled enamel, clawed feet.

Massed trees darken into carbon-paper silhouettes
against the glassy tension of a paling sky
perfecting its spectrum of yellow, mauve and red.

Scarpia's room in the palace. Magnificence.
I can hear Tosca singing. The anguish starts again.

La Traviata in 2001
(for Suzette and Helder)

Hearing the broadcast – a live performance
from the New York Metropolitan Opera –
first in the kitchen, cooking then eating,
then in my study. It has just finished.
So much can happen, while listening to an opera.
The mind inhabits so many parallel worlds.

How angry that story always makes me.
Piange! Piange! The crucial problem:
as angels calmly view the damned soul's torment,
art is also the contemplation of pain's beauty.
The experience is called catharsis. (The same
response can be produced by news reports.)

I was eating, reading the paper, yet listening to Verdi
in a darkened theatre, watching the singers
from somewhere not very close to the stage –
which looks as small as a television screen –
the image distanced, as in a camera's (or a sniper's)
viewfinder, smaller and further away than from
the highest tier of the "gods". Imagined visions
flow into the present's urgent forms.

The tiny, vivid figures gesticulate.
The hollow vessel of the theatre
resonates with instruments and voices.
An audience in thrall – like the poor *traviata*
to Alfredo's love and Germont's power.

I was there in the theatre, also in the kitchen
and in Afghanistan, which I was reading about.
I don't know if – before – minstrels played and sang
comparable romantic sagas there.
Under the burqas are beautiful women;
a grainy agency picture of one of the first to unveil
showed a face with the complex glamour
of a prima donna. And so many handsome fighters:
more than enough protagonists
for a repertoire of tragic operas.

I first heard *Traviata* – Saturday matinee
live from the Met (long may it continue) –
as a schoolgirl in Virginia, at the house
of my opera-struck aunt. Is it possible
that this announcer whose voice sounds so familiar
now, in London fifty years later, could be
the same man who introduced it then?
His description of Violetta's flowered dress
resurrects, yet overlays, the memory
of every Violetta I have seen.

I am listening to an opera, reading an editorial
and thinking about *La Dame aux Camélias*:
remembering how the woman it's based on
always wore a spray of white camellias – except
for those days of the month when she wore one of red.

Dinner is finished and I have moved to my study.
We are each in our study, both radios at full volume
in the almost empty building (it's the weekend before
Christmas, nearly everyone has gone away already)
blaring out Act III – resolution and death – and a friend
in an unhappy marriage has chosen this moment to call.

I can't bring myself to say I don't want to talk
yet surely she can hear the singing behind me.
I haven't lowered the volume, but she only remarks
that she has never understood how
anyone can listen to opera, that caterwauling,
then plunges back into her own story.

Piange, piange, dear friend. Suffering
is a stimulant. A hateful realisation.
Another stratum of thought: that the sexual aspect
of our culture is still unbalanced; and the music
rises to a climactic duet and Violetta's
ecstatic dying words: Joy, joy – it's the end.

My friend wishes me a happy new year.
I listened to her and to Violetta
with equal attention while thinking about
the many different strands of thought
a human brain can plait into the same moment –
and about that film which begins with a man
in a jester's striped red-and-yellow costume, running
through a field of tall grass in northern Italy
in the year nineteen hundred (even though he died
in nineteen hundred and one), shouting, 'Verdi is dead!'

Spiralling

The sigh and scratch and drag
the rustle and swish –
like the hiss of surf
down a shingle beach
as the tide pulls back
and foamy water
slides and sinks
between cold stones, topaz
quartz and malachite,
spiralling – like

the train on a narrow dress
heavy with metal beads,
vitreous glint
and gunmetal glow,
scraping along the floor
then nudged aside by
the tip of a velvet toe
as the music starts
for the next dance
– spiralling.

Shawl

A heap of snow, shovelled
to the side of the road, hardened
by weeks of cold, is netted
in a web of filth like a shawl
of tarnished metal lace
that slid from naked shoulders,
unnoticed, onto the pavement –
to be found and worn till she tore
it or left it in a doorway
by a homeless woman (or did she
drag it from the waste bins
behind an apartment house?).

Such an intricate pattern –
like tire-tracks from that low
slung limousine churning
its wake of freezing slush
and rush of sound: the radio's
raucous blare as a dark
window slides down for a moment
to toss the shawl out, then snaps
back shut, throttling a shout.

What exactly happens
in that smoke-fouled car,
already lost in a murky
vanishing perspective
of tramrails, wires, telephone
lines and blurred neon signs?
– as if the whole district
was deep under water, cruised
by spiniferous creatures
with bulging luminous eyes,
their speckled pleated gills
and accordion-fins swathed
in shredded nets and fringes
of unravelling shawls.

The Constellation of the Jacket

I

The room seemed layered and latticed
with feathers. The faintest movement
of air – a sigh was enough –
would start a slow swirl
of floating feathers:
   receding constellations
   in deep space.

II

He could imagine feathers
glossy as satin ribbons
stitched into a magic jacket
with narrow seams, archaic cut,
   that will never get wet
   always deflect
   arrow, stone or swordstroke

made especially for him:
   youngest son, unacknowledged
   prince – favourite – idiot –
   unwanted one
sent into the world to find his
princess and his palace,
to be a hero,

III

despite the wish
(would he fulfil it?) to refuse
the jacket, deny all duty
to that starry constellation
pattern behind the moon –
   – then open the door wide
   and let a great wind blow through.

The Coloration of Feathers

For glory and brilliance, the colours of feathers
are unsurpassed. Yet the pigments which produce
those shades are few. Some (called subjective
or optical colours) are illusions formed
by the quills' pattern and its achromatic,
horny surface. Is other creatures' vision
of them different, paler or darker, than ours?

Melanin, from blood-plasma or haemoglobin,
makes black, brown and grey; turacin, which fades
when wet, will flush to purple. Darwin wrote
that natives of the Amazonian region
feed fatty fish to green parrots so the lipochromes
will streak them red and yellow (the sacred
tints of royal Inca's feather garments).

Prismatic and metallic tones: blue, gold
and glossy black, are the structural colours.
Only the white lacks underlying pigment.
The evolution of vivid plumage began with
the struggle to win a mate. But the drab hues
of survivors disturb: such complex beauty
unnecessary after that triumph.

Feathers and Jug

Last night I heard the peacocks scream
                              from the park.
This morning I found three feathers
                              on the wet grass.
They are here now, two upright, one
                              curving back
toward the rim of the green and
                              yellow jug
which always stands
                   at the corner of my desk.

The Second Page

The fact that the feathers stretch
from downy base and webby vanes
to speckled tip along the curving
quill, across the two separate panels
of this wide sheet of creamy paper
from the crowded left-hand side

to where their shadows are absorbed
into the empty, sooty darkness (softened
by streaks of light refracted through
a bottle of milky transparence
and a bowl with vitreous-glinting rim)
of the almost empty second page

is more than sufficient matter
to delight in and to contemplate.

The Screen Door

What I remember best
is running up the path
through the humid August dark
past the scary bulk of shrubs
the glow of pallid flowers
drooping and shedding their petals
the exhalation of plants
in neighbours' backyards
watered an hour before:

how I'd vault the wooden steps
push against the screen door's
creaking spring and hinges
onto the shadowy porch
where light from the house, open
from cellar to dormer to any
current of air, diffused,
and the grownups lounged,
too relaxed to talk:

how when the screen door slammed,
from every angle of its
cross-hatched metal mesh
a tiny bead of moisture
iridescent as spray from
the sprinkler, bounced, my face
reflected on its surface
clear as a cameo or
a family portrait: how much
that resemblance confirmed.

My Mother's Eyes

My mother's frightened eyes.
What did she expect?
I never wondered.
In most of the family photos
she is younger than I am –
but seemed an old woman,
already out of the picture.

A picture of my mother.
She wears a fur around her neck
a felt cloche hat with a metal clip
yet isn't elegant.

Maybe it is her posture, hunched,
and the way that handbag is clutched
against her chest,
her frightened eyes.

Every picture of my mother –
alone or with others,
as a young girl or
just before she died –
shows the same wide gaze
desolate and stoic
as a punished child.

When she first saw my baby
and later, during visits
I grudgingly accepted,
her eyes did not alter.

A grandmother's eyes
are meant to show delight,
but the sight of the child
who makes her child a parent
can be another sign
of how little time is left,
of death, not life –

or so I interpret
my mother's expression
in answer to the question
the rankling problem the unsolved
puzzle of what she feared
and expected, as I gaze into
my new-born grandson's eyes.

Even Captain Marvell

My grandchildren are Spiderman and Barbie.
How could they evade the archetypes
any more than I? – who once upon a time
was Wondergirl or even Captain Marvel.

December Moon

Like the web of a leaf – fine as the mesh
of a moth's crest or a filigreed
blade of coral – that I'd stoop to peel
from the damp pavement and carry home
(another object for my collection)
in spite of Mother's protestations

like a scrap of lace on the blue carpet
of her cool bedroom, that lay unnoticed
since I cut and hemmed a veil for my doll
from a torn scarf (or perhaps to knot
around my neck for dressing-up)

like the wrinkled skin my mother would scrape
so carefully with a little spoon
from the top of my cup of boiled milk
(which unless she did I wouldn't drink)

and watch her drop it onto that plate –
my favourite – with a painted line
around the rim like autumn trees
against a sky (it's not that long
since the leaves fell) of the same

rare December blue as the morning sky
I see today here when I draw
the curtains apart, and this pale moon,
half consumed by the last month
of another year, floats into view.

Cousins

The little boy straddles the eldest cousin's shoulders,
silenced by pride.The two of them become
the mythic figure of a Christopher,
a triumphant monster-warrior, a Mayo composite.
Back at ground level, he giggles and
clambers into the basket-crib of his baby sister.

Soft hands pat his naked buttocks and tuck him
under the covers. Petals around a flower's centre,
the cousins cluster and tease:
'Baby, baby, look at the baby.' His eyes like
chips of sapphire slide from one rosy face to another.
He squirms onto his back and grabs his small white penis.

His mother shifts the baby from breast to shoulder.
'You're a big boy now. That's the baby's bed.'
He can tell by all their expressions that it has to end.
He climbs out of the crib and starts to play with
something else, then drops the toy and rushes
across the room, to clutch his father's legs.

Those Days

What were my thoughts, those years
when I had my hair set every week
and wore court shoes with high heels?

The shoe store was on a corner,
opposite 'Your Crowning Glory' –
which seemed important,

though I never knew the reason
why. It was, I recall, the era
I first feared I might reach

a point of no return between possible
alternative futures –
and choose wrong.

Those irrecoverable days
of doubt and joy and pain
were my youth. What more can I say?

Prescience

Long ago, when I was a girl,
constantly, obsessively, I drew
faces of uncertain gender:
philosophers who'd lost conviction,
blocked, bitter artists, or ageing
women with the deep eye-sockets
and bony structures I aspired to,
strong vertical lines marking each
side of a mouth that once was softer,

a face which only now (flinching from
the prospect of what's still to come)
I recognise reflected back
from the mirror – and must acknowledge
the prescience of that young girl
whose hand, as though it held a wicked
fairy's wand or Clotho's spindle and
not a brush or pen, unerringly
created this face, that future.

Brush and Comb

Untwisting hairs from my brush,
tugging them loose, I think
of the cruel princess who stood
on an outspread sheet and charged
her femme-de-chambre to dress
her hair with so much care that
when she stepped off, not one
curl or coil was visible
on the smooth white cloth.

I never imagine being
the princess – always the maid.
I must prefer the role
of victim. (Though sometimes not.)
Best to forget that tale
and use a comb; the shoulders
of my peignoir show
I'm losing too much hair
to my own harsh brush-strokes.

Essential Equipment

The steel stays that pushed through frayed seams from
her grubby corsets – their strange lingerie colours:
soap-greyed white, watery sepia black or
the livid mauve of fading cabbage roses,
and the desert tones: henna, ochre, terra-
cotta, of ointment stains, cosmetic smears
on greasy crumpled tissues and wads of cotton
that blurred her dressing-table's glassy surface;

the enema bag on the back of the bathroom door
its ridged rubber tube and metal clip,
the raw red bulb of her douche syringe and
her shiny leather bunion shield, the tweezers,
scissors, curling tongs like torture instruments;
all those tool and objects – appurtenances
of the female – were the burdens she assumed,
the gear she used: her essential equipment.

Knives

The little mermaid
is stepping on knives,
her song was sacrificed
to gain true love
and win a prince's heart

– knives that carved
two shapely legs
through flashing scales and fins
so she could walk; knives
to mute her tongue.

Now she is halved
to human – woman /
wife / silent one:
roles that she assumed,
knowing the price.

Stranger

Meeting strangers
I lack discrimination
become too familiar
as if greeting a lost relation.

I don't know how to keep my distance
or not feel rebuffed and rejected –
exposed, foolish, pathetic – when
by the second or third occasion
it is perfectly apparent
there is nothing else to say.

I often wonder which one,
in a bus or train, if
disaster came, would pass the test
and save me. Another stranger.

A Picture

A Woolworth picture: wide-eyed brat,
artfully dishevelled, staring through
heavy brushstrokes and dirty scumble
or straight into the camera...

She was just like that: programmed
to charm, tugging your arm, crazy
with need to be reassured that what
she craved was not too much...

Trying to find the right image,
frame it with the best description,
the perfect finishing touch...then
vanish. Step out of the picture.

The Mechanism

Jump off the merry-go-round
whose jangling roar and varnished glare
jolt you awake

Veer out of the path of those plunging
creatures with flaring scarlet nostrils
vacant insect gaze

The whirling sheets of printed paper
rhetoric and propaganda
blown into your face

A desecrated dream-world, gone
from pastoral to derelict
to post-disaster waste

Then force yourself back on and seize
the lever of the mechanism.
Now hard-brake.

In Illo Tempore

(for Ana Maria Pacheco)

The elegant mother, ocelot coat draped
across her shoulders, face masked by a ram's
head with curved gold horns, and the almost
naked daughter in acrobat's regalia
(standing on a box which makes her taller),
their sharp profiles clear against the darkness,
are each holding a burning wire.

One seems to control the brake
of their trolley, the other, the pulley
which keeps that fiery bag suspended
like a token of danger, judgment, fortune,
a god's visitation, floating above them,
lighting their way forward or
blinding them to what is still to come.

SHEBA AND SOLOMON

I *Their Words*

A dark winter day. The end of an afternoon.
A young girl sits in the empty school library
reading *Solomon's Song*. She thinks of an orchard:
almond / apple / etrog / pomegranate / fig.
She stares down at the whorled grain of the table,
the same pattern there on her fingertips,
and reads again: 'My beloved is unto me as
a cluster of camphire in the vineyards of En-Gedi.'
She sees a fountain, its jets and conduits,
the marble basin carved with rampant lions
and dragon-headed cherubim. Around it
grow flowers and spices: crocus / roses / lilies.
'I am my beloved's, and my beloved is mine:
he feedeth among the lilies.' The words disturb
and excite. Myrrh / spikenard / frankincense.
Her whole body goes icy-hot, imagining
that caress. Under sleeves and stockings,
at the back of her neck, the soft hairs lift.

II *The Hoopoe*

Imagine somewhere so far from Jerusalem
not even the Temple-builder Solomon
knew about that country with a queen.

When the hoopoe, to excuse her absence
from the canopy which all the birds of the air
formed to shade the king's head

and save herself from cruel punishment
or execution, explained she had found
a place where a woman ruled

and the One God was not yet worshipped,
Solomon gasped with disbelief.
He had to see this woman.

III *Solomon*

Solomon understood the language of birds.
He spoke with animals. Djinns obeyed him,
angels praised his words.

He had seen heaven and gehenna, earth's molten
matrix, had watched the elements transmute
and fuse into gold.

He knew the secrets of life and death. No man
knew as much. He had been a shaman.
He had been a woman.

    *

When Solomon needed water, he summoned
his hoopoe, who could see through sand and rock
the secret rivers running underground.

Where the hoopoe marked the place with her beak
(her beak marked with the name of God) his servants
dug, and drew sweet water for Solomon.

IV *Sheba's Marriage*

Sheba despised the local princelings, as
her haughty father, King of all the Yemen,
rejected human women and chose a demon's
daughter for wife. With such a mother, Sheba
would not accept a life of spinning cloth,
weaving carpets – nor submit to marriage.
She was born to be the natural successor.
But for reasons of tactics, and to gain
the tribes' allegiance, she needed a consort.

Courtiers and nobles found it hard to accept
the one Sheba proposed. He also was astonished,
shamed (fearing refusal) not to have spoken
first, as the man should. She talked about
passion and acted besotted, rolled her eyes
and grinned. He was so easy to deceive.
Later, alone, the moment before he could touch her
or understood what was happening, she reached
for the hidden sword – and then moved closer.

V *The Invitation*

Sheba worshipped the sun,
but sight of the rising god
was blocked that day by the hoopoe
who perched in her eastern window
bearing Solomon's letter,
an invitation – or command –
to visit him. How could
a woman so sceptical
worship what disappears each
night, is eclipsed by a bird?

Sheba got her husband drunk
on their wedding night, then cut off his head
and hung it from the palace gate.
She had no problem after that –
until Solomon's hoopoe opened its beak
and dropped a letter on her neck
in the same place the sword had struck.
His words were as smooth as his penmanship,
but she sensed a threat. She sought advice
from her wisest men – and then ignored it.

VI *Sheba's Tests*

First she sent him treasure.
If he kept it, like any lesser king,
that would prove her the stronger.
When he sent it back, she understood
he was a man of power.
Yet she had to test him further.

*

She sent five hundred girls
five hundred boys, dressed in each others' clothes
to try his subtlety and intuition
to see if he would notice.

She sent an unpierced pearl
a moonstone hollowed in a twisted spiral.
Was one a symbol of virginity
the other, of violation?

*

When he solved her riddles –
could not be deceived by disguise, but recognised
the difference between the children,
the essence of male and female

and, to meet her challenge,
commanded that an earthworm and a fruitworm
pierce the pearl and thread the moonstone –
she confirmed his wisdom
> and went herself.

VII *Sheba's Journey*

Once she had decided to accept his invitation, Sheba ordered her
caravan to be assembled outside the walls of Kitor. There were
horses, camel-trains and teams of asses with their grooms and
drivers, soldiers and courtiers and all their servants, her advisers
and attendants. They were thousands.

This is the list of gifts for Solomon:
brilliant-plumaged birds and pearls from Kamaran island, where
> the divers go in the cool of dawn to the oyster banks, then
> under the shade of sails from their dhows rigged on sticks
> in the sand, sing and play their drone and pipes through
> the hot afternoon
myrrh and frankincense from Hajja and Suda
translucent flasks of alabaster oozing perfume: spikenard and benzoin
> and terebinth
jars of honey from the hives of Hadramhaut
fragile rolls of cinnamon and cassia bark
robes and carpets woven from the silky hair of mountain goats and
> fleeces from her finest flocks
silver chains and artefacts of gold from the mines south of Taif:
> brooches, bracelets, buttons, earrings, necklaces and pins;
> tripods, boxes, goblets and bowls, the best examples of
> her craftsmens' skills, carefully packed and crated into the
> great baskets for which the region was famous.
It took more than three months for all to be made ready.

Once they set out on their journey, this is what they saw:
the great dam of Marib, its walls so tall and grand, the story was
> it had been built by giants
granite peaks of the desert range

shafts of purple light between bare yellow crags
red volcanic cones and dark grey lava fields
strata of pale marl and black basalt columns
the vapour of hot springs rising from craters
piled towers of cloud, thunder and hail, cold or burning winds
a mountain that glittered, as if clothed in mail, after a heavy rainstorm
dry and flooded wadis in their different seasons
scorpions, vipers, awl-headed snakes to avoid
bustard, quail and larks to soothe their eyes
hedgehogs and foxes, jerbils and spiny mice, the smallest desert
      creatures
gazelles and lions
sandstone monoliths eroded by windblown grit
salt mines and rocky ground brittle with iron ore
endless dunes of the empty quarter, the horizon shifting like a slowly
      flicking whip
the rare oases
blasts of heat from sun-scorched stone and sand
glare bounced back by every smooth surface
brilliant starlight and moonlight after vivid sunsets, the maw and
      roaring furnace of the fiery heavens.

Through all the seasons, Sheba and her retinue moved northward
over mountain passes, into shadowed valleys between massifs, across
dusty tilted tableland and unmarked desert, until at last they reached
a low, monotonous, pebbled shore. This was the border of Solomon's
kingdom. A final climb through the Judaean hills would bring them
to Jerusalem.

VIII   *Sheba and the Trees*

When Sheba entered Jerusalem
with her gaudy, caparisoned caravan, she
stopped at the bridge on the river, refused
to put one foot on that sacred timber,
but bowed down and wept and worshipped it.
They say that Sheba was the link between
Adam and Jesus. This is what they tell.

Like the ripest fruit on the tree of life,
dying Jesus hung on a cross
of wood from the great tree on Adam's grave:

72

tree sprung from the seed of a fruit of the same
tree that gave knowledge of good and evil,
the fruit Seth begged from the fiery angel
who stood at the gate of empty Eden.
To taste that fruit again, its mingled flavours
of death and sin and pleasure,
was his dying father's last wish.

The germinating seed split Adam's coffin
and grew to be the noblest tree in Judea.
Centuries later, King Solomon,
building his Temple, had the tree felled.
But the beam hewn from its trunk was rejected
by the workmen, and used instead
as a bridge across the Kedron river.

Some tell how Sheba warned Solomon
of the sorrow his race was doomed to suffer
and therefore wept, how she revealed
that the tree which would redeem mankind
was the same by which all had been damned:
the tree from which the beam was cut.
Solomon believed each word she said.
He had it carried to the Temple's
Treasure House, to wait the hour
her prophecy should be fulfilled.

IX *Their Meeting*

Solomon sat on a crystal throne
as wide and tall as an elephant
on the far side of a glittering court
which his djinns had conjured in less
than a moment, its glass floor invisible
above a pool of clear cool water.

When he beckoned her close, Sheba
approached, dazzled by such splendour,
but wary. Why were fishes swimming
there between them? Thinking to keep
its fine threads dry, she slowly raised
the hem of her embroidered skirt.

Solomon stared. The tale was true –
she was only half-human, an efreet's child,
with the face of a girl but the hirsute legs
of a youth. 'You're beautiful,' he said,
'but this is wrong. Here in my kingdom,
women and men must be different.'

X *The Sweat of Horses*

In this story, glass and water
signify deceit. Sheba's riddle
is: what water comes neither
from below the earth nor falls from heaven?
One answer: the sweat of horses.
Horses and water are the desert's wealth.
(Another answer: the tears of women.)

Water beneath the glassy floor
of Solomon's court, where he sat on his throne
like a painted pope, was meant to confuse,
so she would lift her robe to show
pelted feet and ankles, smooth
as the coat of a fine horse. (But
Sheba never wept for Solomon.)

XI *Water*

Through transparencies of water
like shifting panels of broken glass,
rocking reflections of golden carp
fins swirling out then narrowing
like fans, Solomon imagines
Sheba's ankles as if she stood
in a stream immersed to the knee –
how a film of air would coat her legs
with silver stockings, and a cluster
of bubbles cling to each hair along
the shin around hard-muscled calves
like a sheath of seed pearls.

XII *Solomon's Desire*

Her name is a red word like a red flame to burn the tongue
        that speaks it.
The bitter rust of desire is eating my breast. It is blinding
        my eyes with red dust.

Sheba among the women is a vine plant among acanthus.
Sheba among the women is a date palm among wild plum trees.
Sheba among the women is a cypress in a grove of tamarisk.

Her voice is a jet of water lifting to the sky, a river falling
        among the rocks.
For her I would climb the black mountain of the sky from peak
        to peak and pluck the lily of the moon and the stars' buds.
She is silver and gold hammered together.
She is the wine of my mouth, the water of the well preferred,
        the cleansing and assuaging water.

She is a statue of white salt, the fringes of red belts, she is
        my carpet of dark wool, my bright fountain, my cool garden.
She is like the naked summer moon. Her beauty is hot as amber.
Her jewels press blue and crimson kisses upon her body. My lips
        will double their number.
The wet fruit of her mouth. Her skin as soft as bread.

I desire her as the sky desires the mountain, as the mountain
        the plain, as a new-sown field the first rain.
All the men who passed their turn in her bed are no more to me
        than clouds passing before the moon.
And all my wives and concubines are no more to me than vapours
        of the dew to the sun who makes them.

XIII *Sheba's Mistakes*

What were Sheba's three mistakes?

The first mistake:
When Sheba stopped outside the walls of Jerusalem,
Solomon sent water to wash away the dust of the road
and an envoy to receive her. Dazzled by the young man's
beauty and splendour, she thought he was the King himself.

The second mistake:
When, to prove the story false or true
that the Queen's legs showed a growth of hair like a goat or
an ass or a demon, Solomon used his magic arts to confuse her
so she would see the floor of his court as a pool –
Sheba raised her skirts to wade through the water.

The third mistake:
When Solomon made her swear that if she took even
one thing of his, he might come to her bed – then
fed her spicy meat and potent wine so she would thirst –
she did not think a single cup of water broke that oath.
But, 'What is more precious than water?' he asked,
and claimed the right to do as he wished.

XIV *They Break Their Oath*

Solomon slept with eyes half open,
but when he was awake he closed them.
No one guessed that, like a spy,
he could watch whatever they did. Sheba,
who had eaten and drunk too much
and only reluctantly agreed
to share his chamber, was amazed.
He seemed to fall asleep at once.

Hours later, the queen lay wakeful
and thirsty. She'd forgotten their oath.
All she craved was a sip from the jug
he'd filled with cool water then placed
between them, its curving sides slick
with oozing moisture. Her only thought

was not to disturb him. She moved across
the darkened room as soft as a cat.

Runnels of delicious water
trickled down her throat and damped
her robe; then she gasped, spluttered,
choked, to feel one hand clutch
her hip and another, her breast.
The dropped jug shattered like shrapnel
and sprayed them both as Solomon groaned
and pulled her onto his bed.

XV *In Solomon's Garden*

Under bright clusters on a grape arbour, silvery
leaves of the oldest olive tree in Jerusalem
and the thrashing shadow of the tallest date-palm,
Sheba and Solomon lounged by a great pool
thick with white and yellow water-lilies, sipping
pomegranate juice and admiring his garden.

She'd brought roots from her own orchards: storax
and cistus, whose bark exudes a balsam for incense.
He'd plant them near the almond tree (its pale wood
made Aaron's rod, its pale flowers resemble seven-
branched candelabra), the myrtles and oleanders used
for Tabernacle booths to celebrate the harvest.

'Your kisses are the drowsy juice of white poppies,
your scent the essence of jasmine and narcissi, you are
as beautiful as scarlet tulips from Galilee.' But then
he teased: 'Look where that hyssop grows from the wall.
Its sharp berries and dark shaggy stamens are like
the taste of your nipples, and my first sight of your legs.'

XVI *Legends of Sheba*

Sheba was called Balkis in Yemen;
by the cabbalists, Lilith,
riddle-poser, dark sister
of the Shekinah; in Abyssinia
Candace or Makeda the Southern Queen.

She was named the mother of many:
Nebuchadnezzar, who wrecked
his father's Temple; the magus kings
who worshipped Yahweh's son;
and Menelik, first Lion of Judah.

Like a sibyl, Sheba
prophesied the coming of Christ.
A pagan, yet she foretold
Islam's triumph. She acknowledged
Solomon's true wisdom.

Thirty silver coins
among the gifts she brought
to Solomon, were looted
from the Temple's treasure
house by Nebuchadnezzar,

but reappeared
as the same ones offered
to Jesus by the three wise men;
then played a further part in
the story as payment to Judas.

And always, in every legend,
those hairy legs.

XVII *Another Version*

Queen Makeda and her dear friend Sawneth,
like jaunty girls craving adventure,
set out from Tigré and sailed up the Red Sea
to the tip of Sinai to learn for themselves
if all they had heard of the wealth and wisdom
of great King Solomon was really true.

Makeda braided her hair to look like a man,
Sawneth did the same.They helped each other
wrap the thick dark plaits around their heads
and tuck them under long-fringed shawls,
placed the jewelled coronet, then tenderly
smoothed damask robes over bound breasts,
shoulders and back. Now they were ready

to enter Jerusalem in regal splendour
as King of Abyssinia and his Prime Minister.

Because they ate and drank so little
at the welcome-banquet, Solomon guessed
they were women. That night, he tricked them
with a bowl of honey and watched them lick it
when they thought he slept. From one bed
to the next he crept, without a word
embraced them both, one after the other.
Makeda laughed, and Sawneth shouted:
'My deflowering has been accomplished!'

Solomon gave the queen a silver mirror
as a parting gift, so wonderful
she thought it had been made by demon smiths.
Years later, she gave it to Menelik,
'Son of the Wise', when he set out –
with Sawneth's boy as his companion –
to find the place of his conception,
present himself at last to Solomon.

Makeda knew how devious
the king could be. But once he saw
his own reflection: Menelik,
his replica and image – though Solomon
might hide among his courtiers
or wear disguise to test the boy, she
was quite sure the son would recognise
his father, the father not deny
his own blood, and her flesh.

Menelik stole the Ark of the Covenant
from the Sanctuary of Solomon's Temple,
then persuaded twelve young Israelites
from the oldest priestly families
to follow him across the desert and
beyond the mountains to Ethiopia:
a rebellious farewell. His kingdom
would become the second Zion,
and he, Makeda's cub, be Judah's lion.

XVIII *Hair*

Why was Solomon obsessed with body hair? (No more obsessed than I.) The pelt on Sheba's legs connects, like the strands of a web, so many points and tender nodes of the past: resurrects the shame and pride of those curled tendrils in armpit and groin, the fascination with hairy moles on my father's neck; my aunt's warning not to shave my legs or the hairs would thicken and coarsen, I'd be forced to do it forever. Hard to imagine forever. Of course I ignored her. All my friends, the girls in my class, set the example. But under strata of rebellion and conformity lay the half-conscious, dubious pleasure of being stupid. It overpowered me then; only now can I understand what was happening: collusion with the process of becoming a woman.

Solomon knew that until Sheba accepted his demons' depilatory formula (she was their first client), and unless she submitted to such symbolic gelding – to put it bluntly – she would not be appropriate for his attentions. He lusted for her, but those legs were too much like a man's. It was a problem.

I am sure that ceremony did not seem very important to Sheba. The novelty of being smooth, like the nights that followed, had been part of it all, another among the memories she pondered, later, back home in Ethiopia, with Menelik at her breast – or was it the Yemen, and Nebuchadnezzar? The skin felt rough and itched when the hairs pushed through, but then the bristles lengthened and softened. (My aunt was right but also wrong.) She preferred her legs like this.